First Book of Pop

Popular Christmas • Popular Hits • Popular Praise

32 Arrangements for Beginning Pianists

With Optional Teacher/Parent Accompaniments

Gayle Kowalchyk • E. L. Lancaster • Christine H. Barden

Produced by
Alfred Music
P.O. Box 10003
Van Nuys, CA 91410-0003
alfred.com

ISBN-10: 0-7390-9068-2
ISBN-13: 978-0-7390-9068-8

Foreword

Young piano students enjoy playing familiar music. FIRST BOOK OF POP was designed for those students who are just beginning to read music notation.

POSITIONS: Melodies for the pieces are divided between the hands. All positions are shown on the page with the notation. Most melodies remain within a single position, but some use accidentals that require movement out of the position. These sharps or flats apply to the rest of the measure.

RHYTHM: Students may be unfamiliar with the rhythmic notation of some of the pieces. However, they will usually play the music correctly by memory or, if not, the rhythms can be quickly learned by rote.

ACCOMPANIMENTS: Each piece in the book has a duet accompaniment. The accompaniments give the pieces richer sounds and can aid the student with rhythmic security. These pieces make excellent student/teacher or student/parent duets. Both solo and accompaniment parts contain measure numbers for easy reference.

Table of Contents

Mickey Mouse March

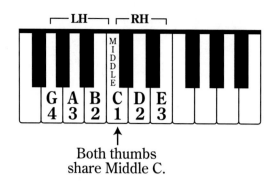

Both thumbs
share Middle C.

Words and Music by Jimmie Dodd
Arr. by Kowalchyk, Lancaster, and Barden

Who's the lead-er of the club that's

made for you and me!

Duet Accompaniment: Student plays one octave higher.

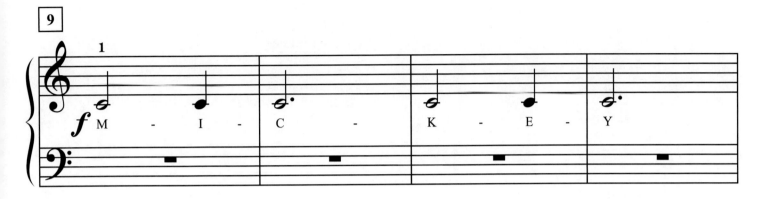

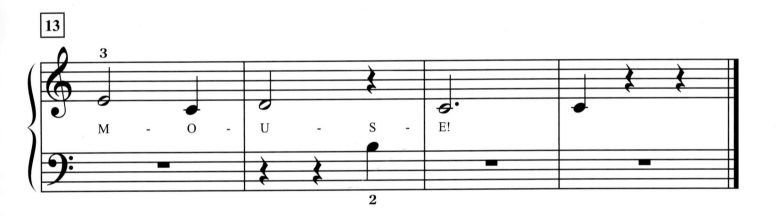

6

Winnie the Pooh

(from Walt Disney's *"The Many Adventures of Winnie the Pooh"*)

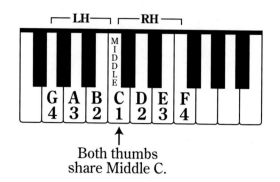

Both thumbs
share Middle C.

Words and Music by
Richard M. Sherman and Robert B. Sherman
Arr. by Kowalchyk, Lancaster, and Barden

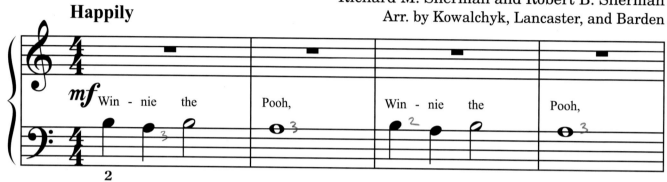

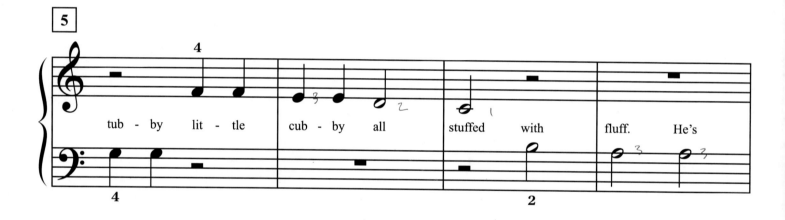

Duet Accompaniment: Student plays one octave higher.

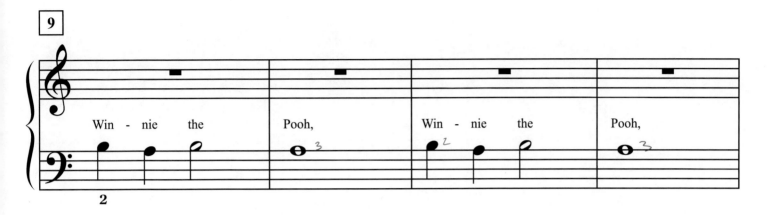

8

Puff (the Magic Dragon)

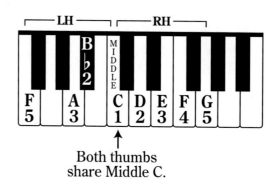

Both thumbs
share Middle C.

Words and Music by
Peter Yarrow and Leonard Lipton
Arr. by Kowalchyk, Lancaster, and Barden

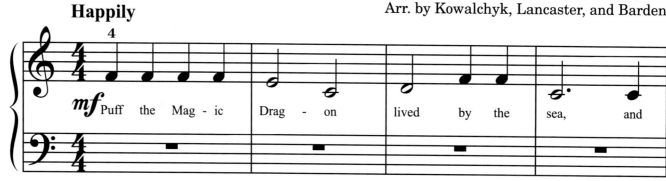

Happily

Puff the Mag - ic Drag - on lived by the sea, and

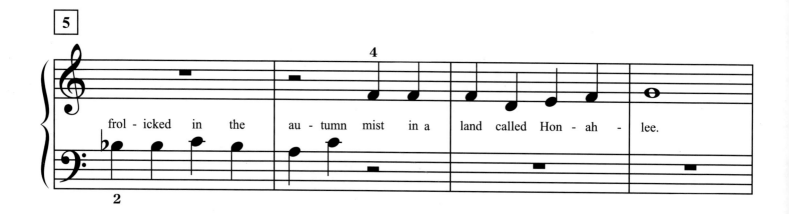

frol - icked in the au - tumn mist in a land called Hon - ah - lee.

Duet Accompaniment: Student plays one octave higher.

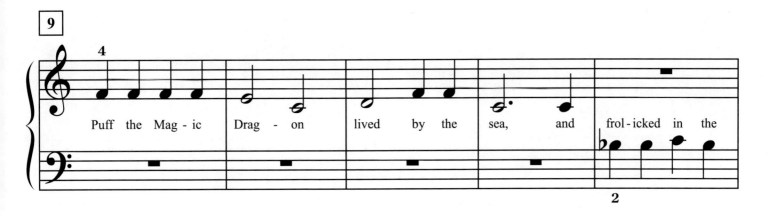

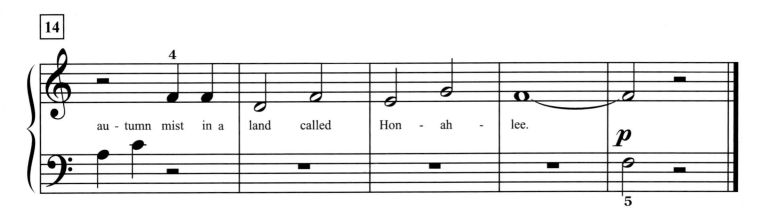

If I Only Had a Brain

(from the M-G-M Motion Picture
The Wizard of Oz)

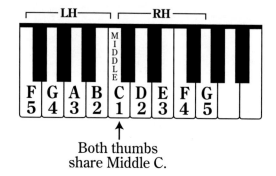

Both thumbs
share Middle C.

Music by Harold Arlen
Lyric by E. Y. Harburg
Arr. by Kowalchyk, Lancaster, and Barden

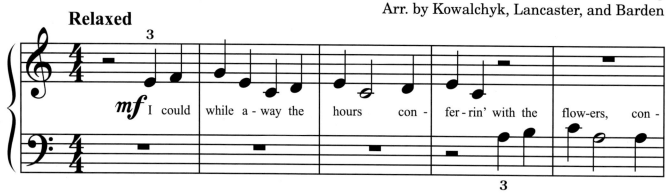

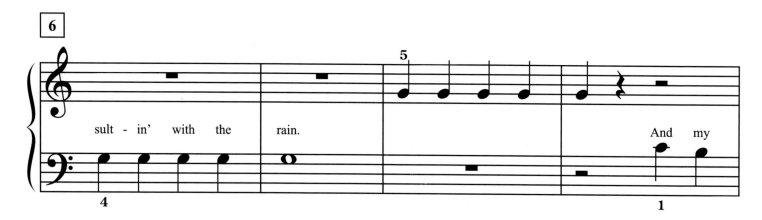

Duet Accompaniment: Student plays one octave higher.

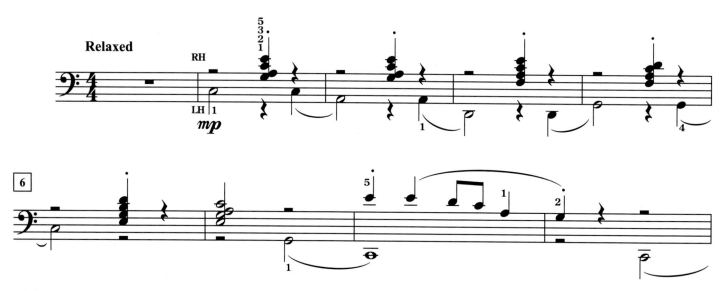

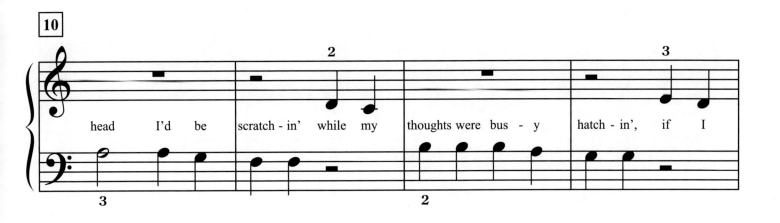

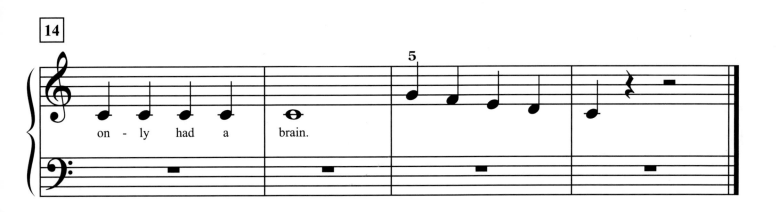

Hooray for Hollywood

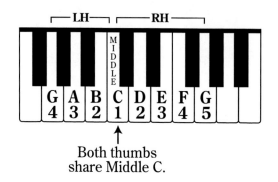

Both thumbs
share Middle C.

Words by Johnny Mercer
Music by Richard A. Whiting
Arr. by Kowalchyk, Lancaster, and Barden

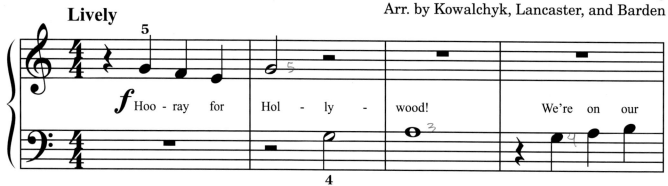

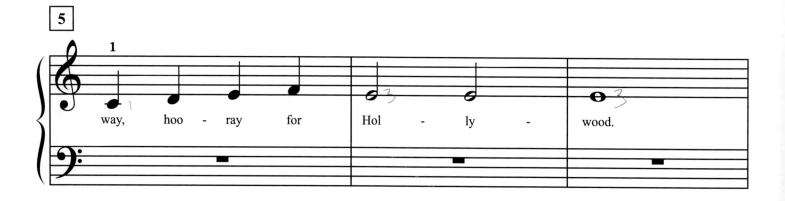

Duet Accompaniment: Student plays one octave higher.

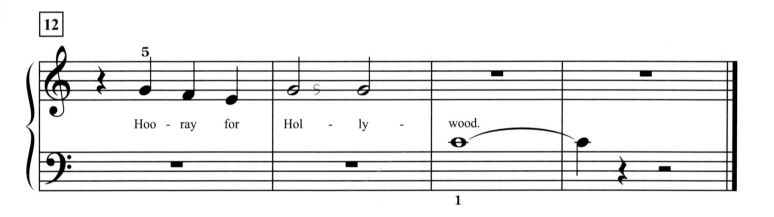

Star Wars
(Main Theme)

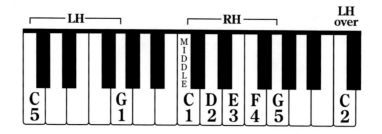

Music by JOHN WILLIAMS
Arr. by Kowalchyk, Lancaster, and Barden

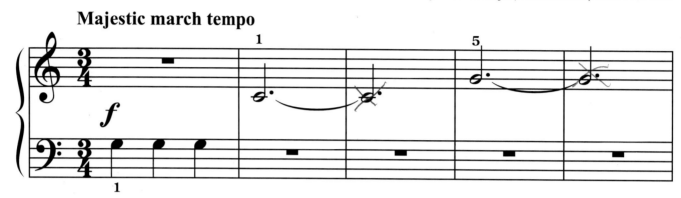

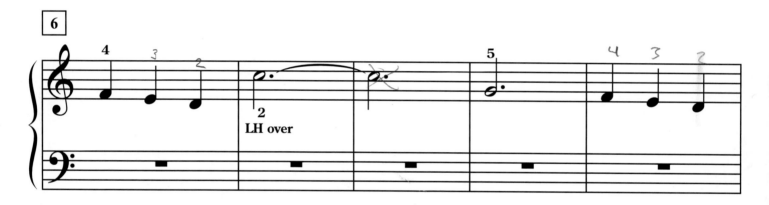

Duet Accompaniment: Student plays one octave higher.

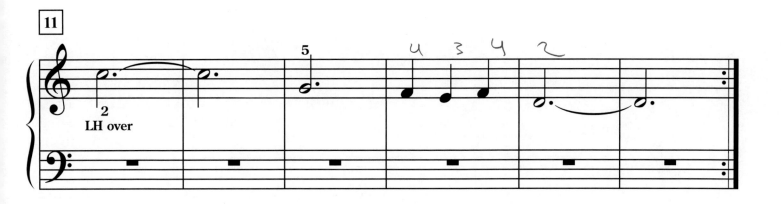

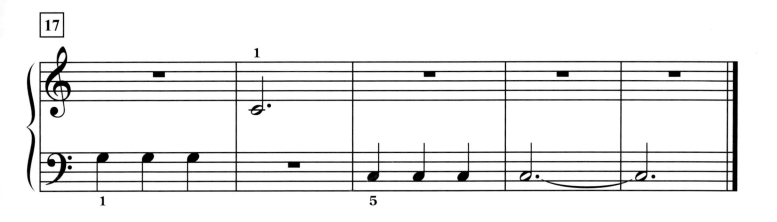

(Meet) The Flintstones

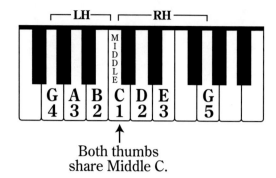

Words and Music by
Joseph Barbera, William Hanna, and Hoyt Curtin
Arr. by Kowalchyk, Lancaster, and Barden

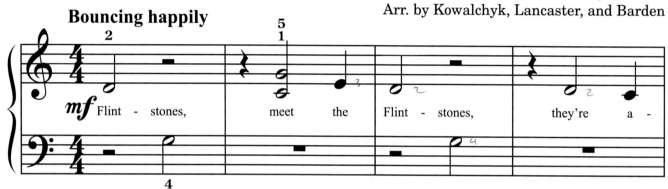

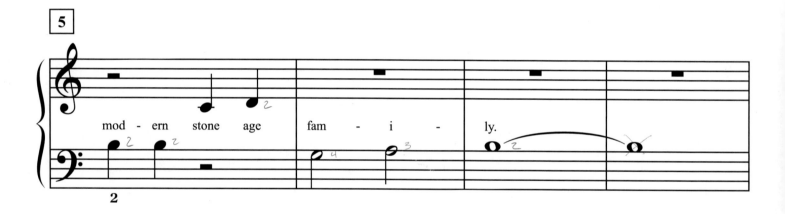

Duet Accompaniment: Student plays one octave higher.

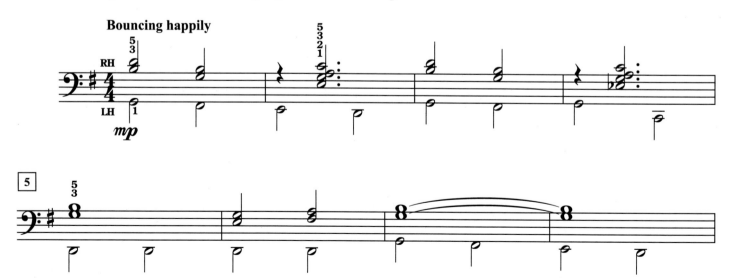

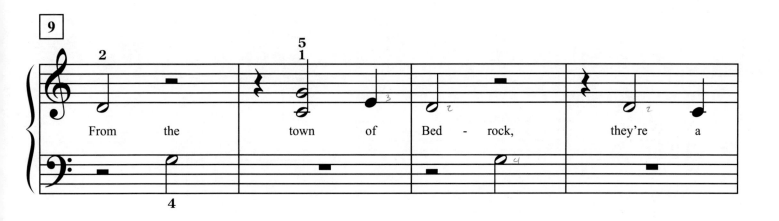

From the   town   of   Bed - rock,   they're   a

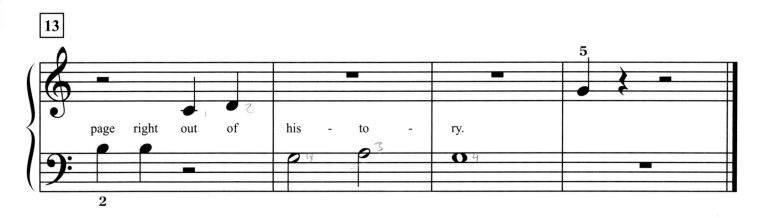

page   right   out   of   his - to - ry.

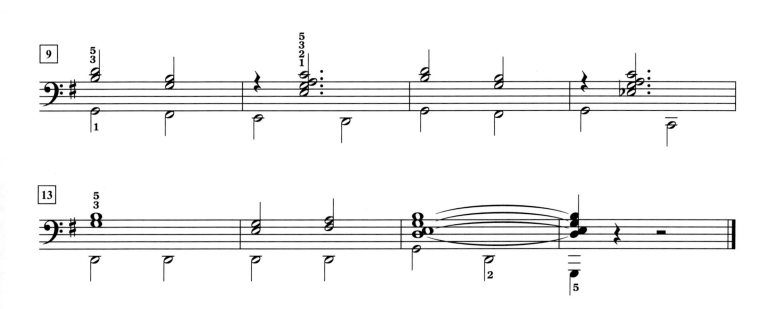

Over the Rainbow

(from the M-G-M Motion Picture
The Wizard of Oz)

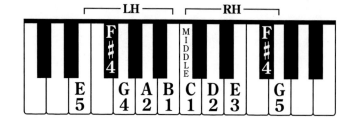

Music by Harold Arlen
Lyric by E. Y. Harburg
Arr. by Kowalchyk, Lancaster, and Barden

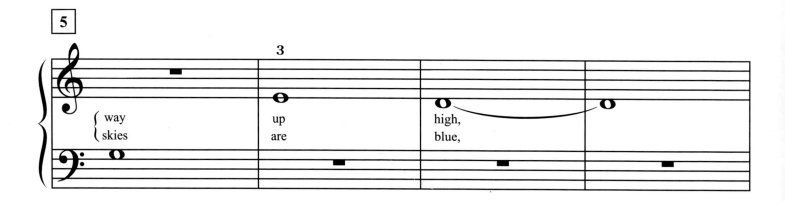

Duet Accompaniment: Student plays one octave higher.

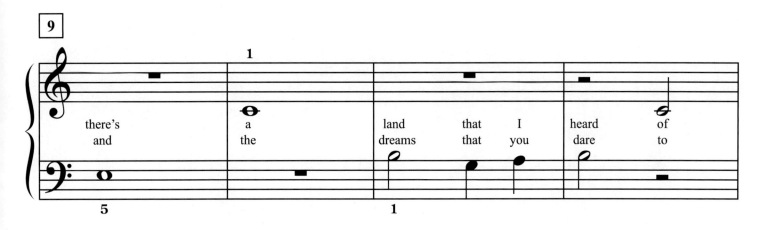

Supercalifragilistic-expialidocious

(from Walt Disney's *"Mary Poppins"*)

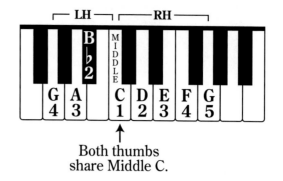

Both thumbs
share Middle C.

Words and Music by
Richard M. Sherman and Robert B. Sherman
Arr. by Kowalchyk, Lancaster, and Barden

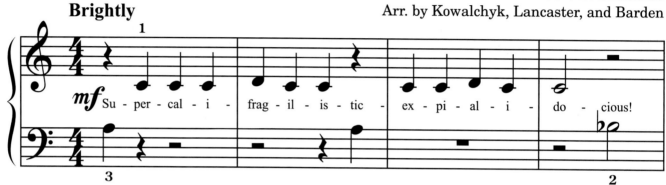

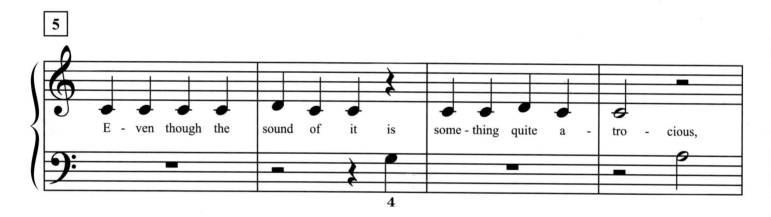

Duet Accompaniment: Student plays one octave higher.

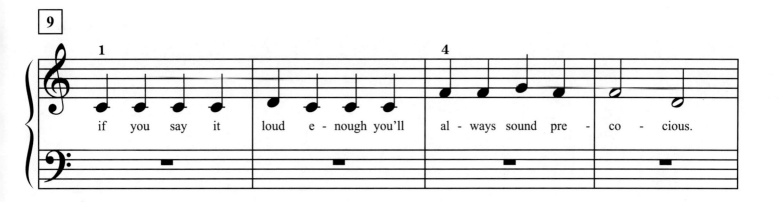

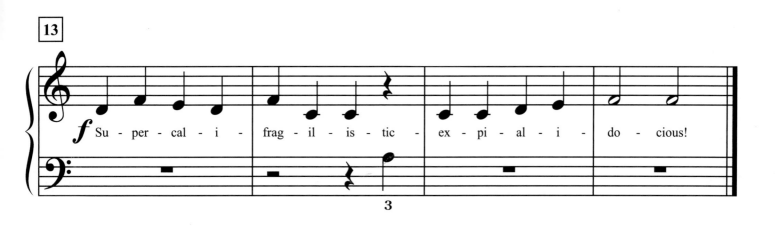

Itsy Bitsy Teenie Weenie Yellow Polka Dot Bikini

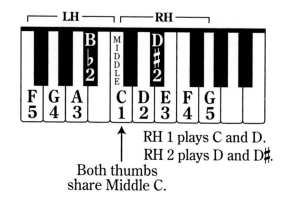

RH 1 plays C and D.
RH 2 plays D and D♯.
Both thumbs
share Middle C.

Words and Music by
Paul J. Vance and Lee Pockriss
Arr. by Kowalchyk, Lancaster, and Barden

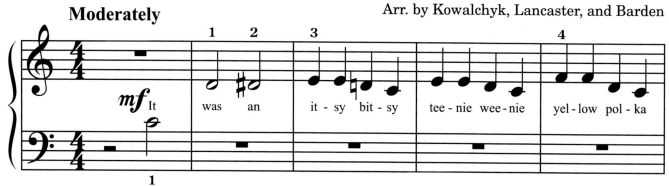

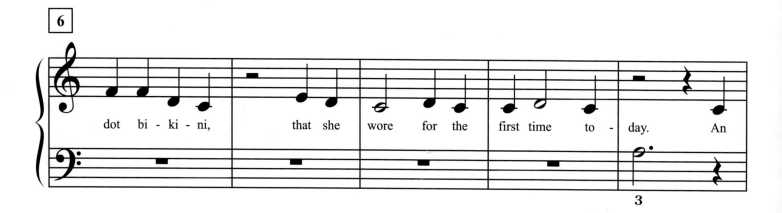

Duet Accompaniment: Student plays one octave higher.

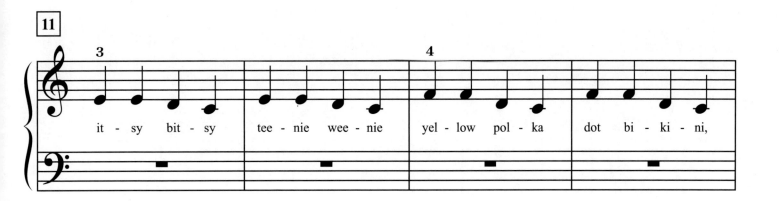

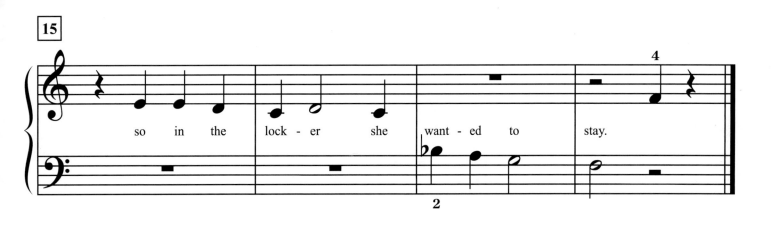

It's a Small World

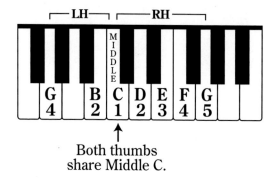

Both thumbs
share Middle C.

Words and Music by
Richard M. Sherman and Robert B. Sherman
Arr. by Kowalchyk, Lancaster, and Barden

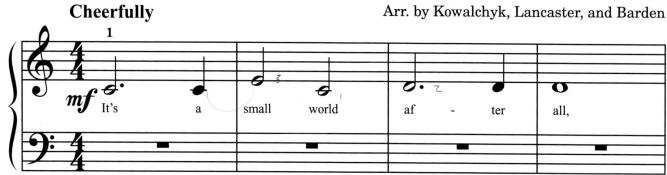

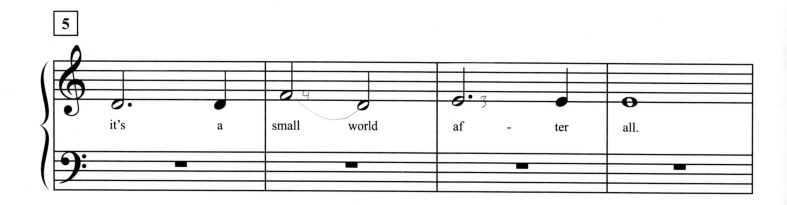

Duet Accompaniment: Student plays one octave higher.

It's a small world af - ter all, it's a

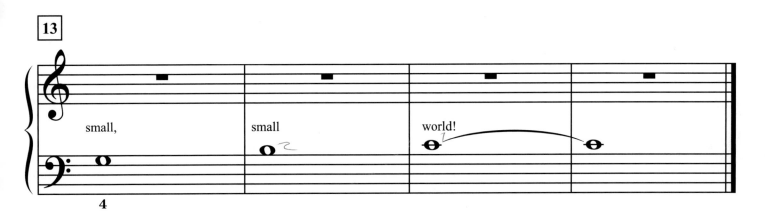

small, small world!

This Land Is Your Land

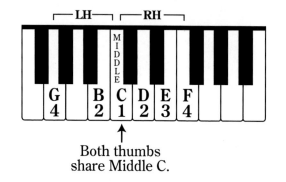

Both thumbs
share Middle C.

Words and Music by Woody Guthrie
Arr. by Kowalchyk, Lancaster, and Barden

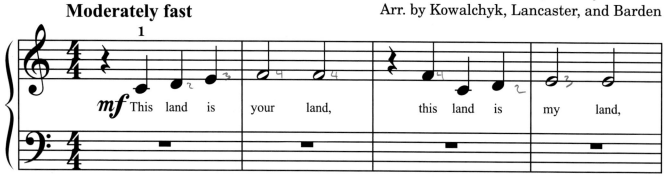

Duet Accompaniment: Student plays one octave higher.

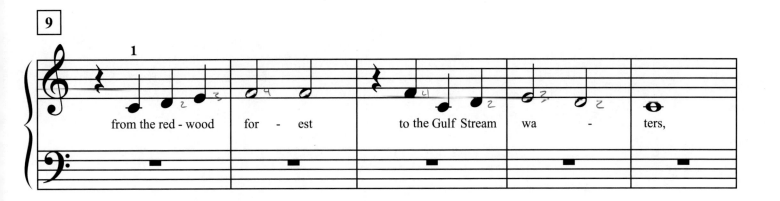

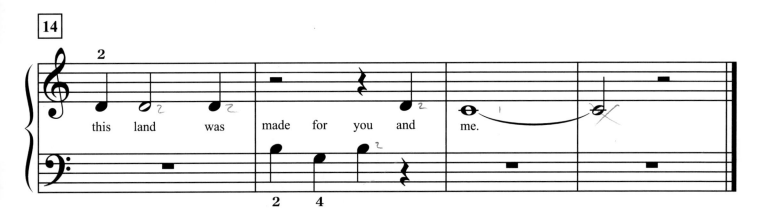

The Lion Sleeps Tonight

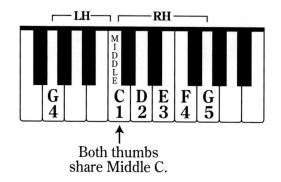

New Lyric and Revised Music by
George David Weiss, Hugo Peretti, and Luigi Creatore
Arr. by Kowalchyk, Lancaster, and Barden

Moderate, with courage

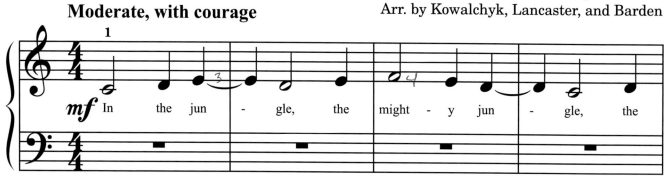

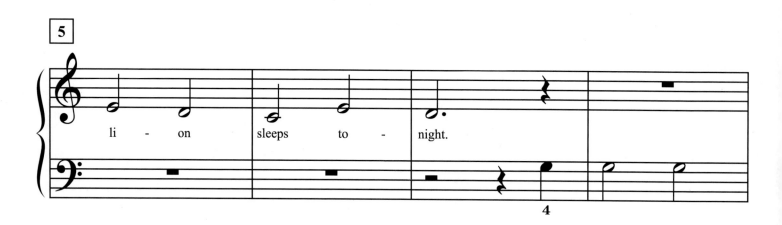

Duet Accompaniment: Student plays one octave higher.

Moderate, with courage

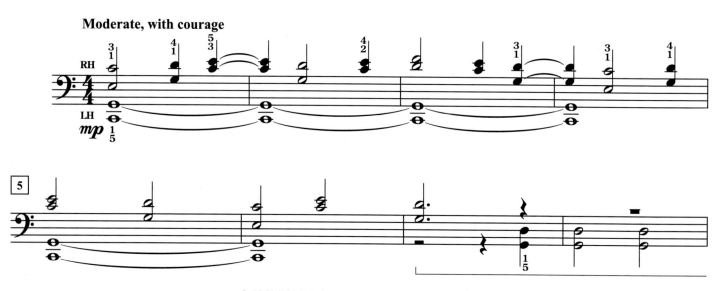

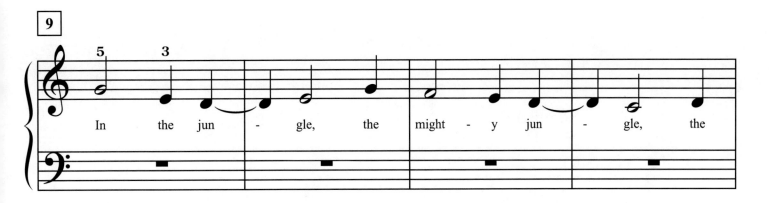

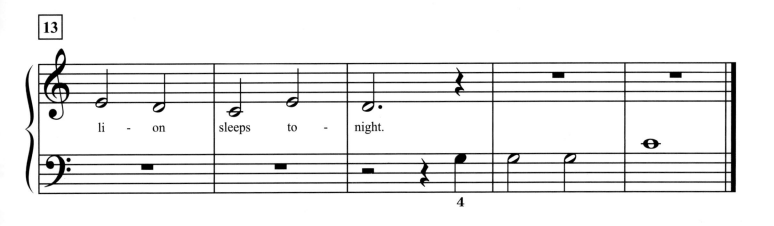

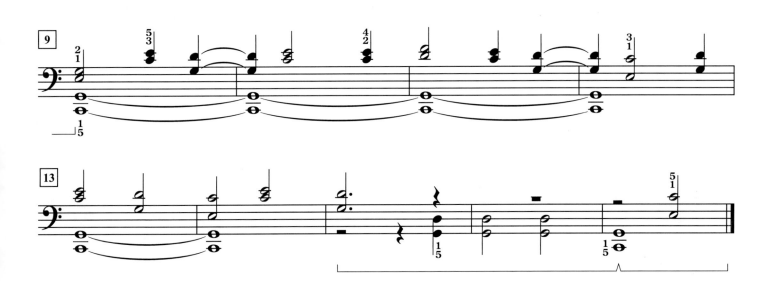

The Chicken Dance
(Dance Little Bird)

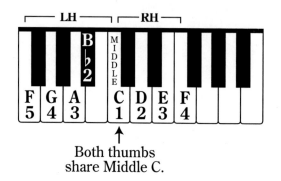

Both thumbs
share Middle C.

Music by Terry Rendall and Werner Thomas
English Lyrics by Paul Parnes
Arr. by Kowalchyk, Lancaster, and Barden

Fast and clucky

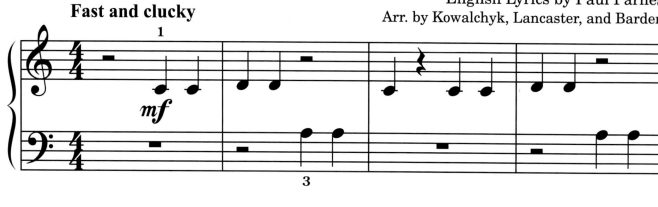

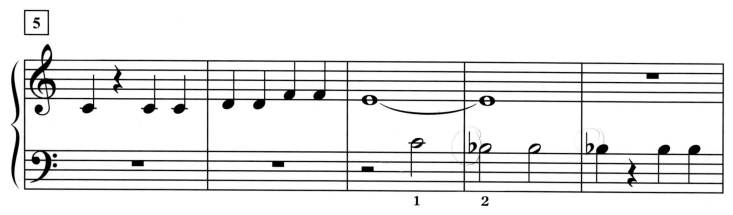

Duet Accompaniment: Student plays one octave higher.

Fast and clucky
quarter notes detached

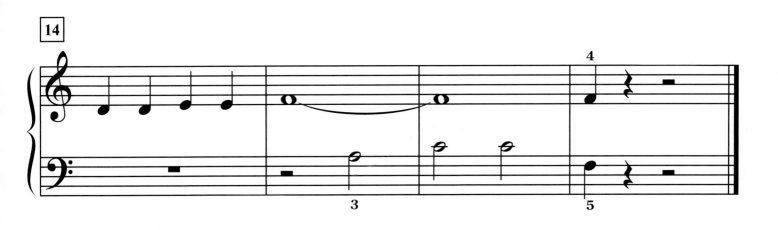

Inspector Gadget
(Main Title)

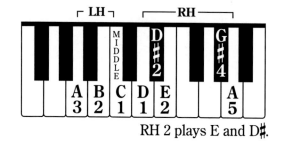

RH 2 plays E and D♯.

Words and Music by
Haim Saban and Shuki Levy
Arr. by Kowalchyk, Lancaster, and Barden

Moving fast!

Duet Accompaniment: Student plays one octave higher.

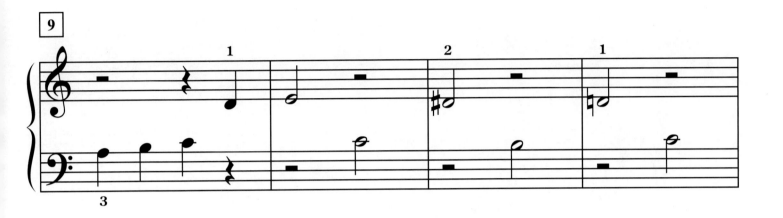

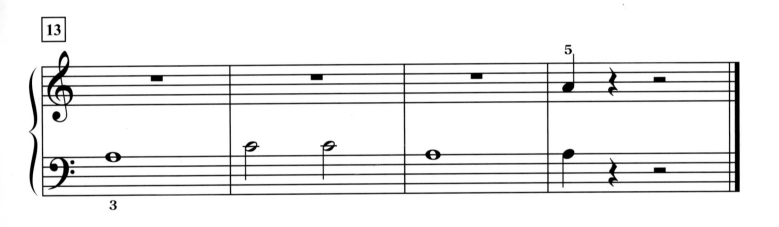

Theme from "Superman"

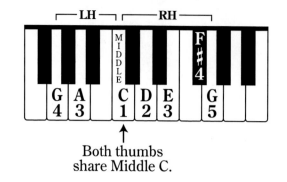

Both thumbs
share Middle C.

By JOHN WILLIAMS
Arr. by Kowalchyk, Lancaster, and Barden

Moderately fast

Duet Accompaniment: Student plays one octave higher.

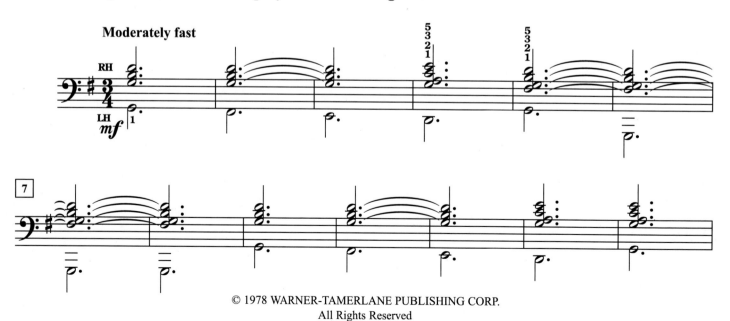

The Imperial March
(Darth Vader's Theme)

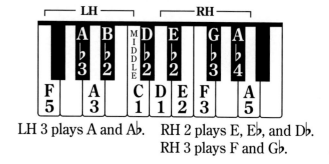

LH 3 plays A and A♭.   RH 2 plays E, E♭, and D♭.
RH 3 plays F and G♭.

By JOHN WILLIAMS
Arr. by Kowalchyk, Lancaster, and Barden

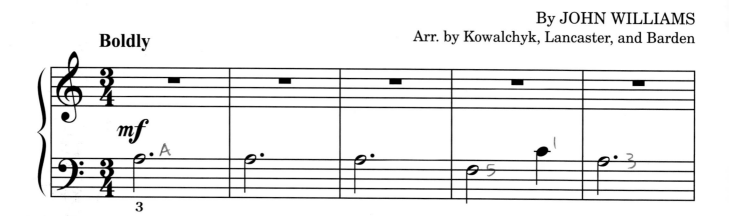

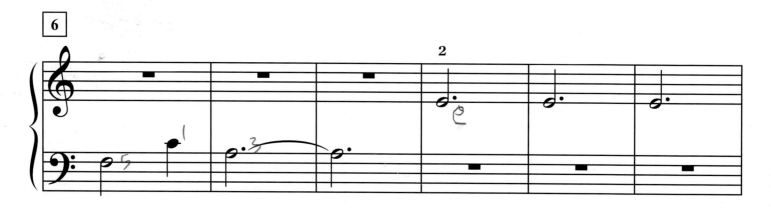

Duet Accompaniment: Student plays one octave higher.

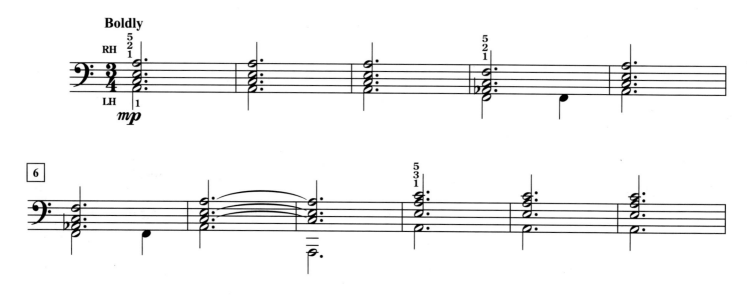

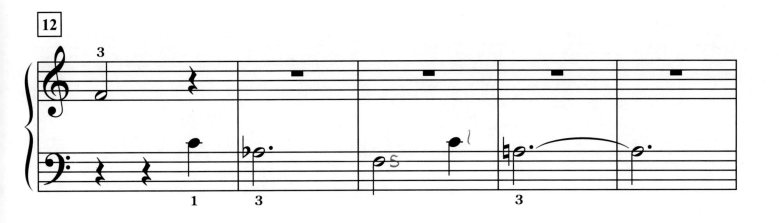

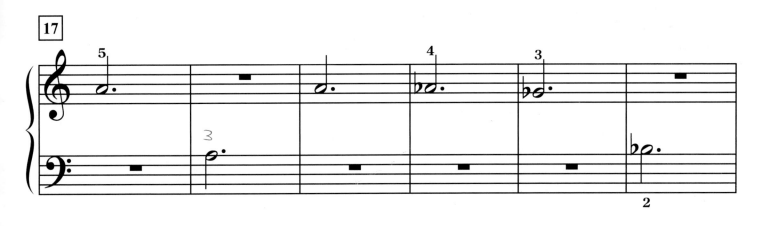

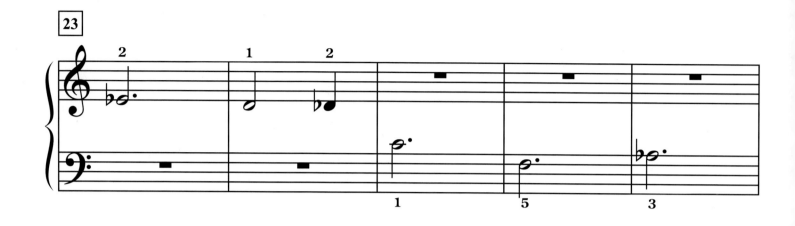

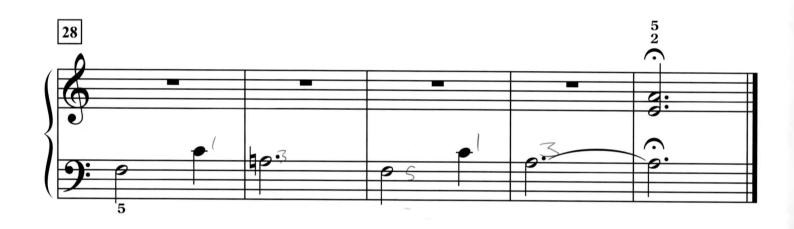

Here I Am to Worship
(Light of the World)

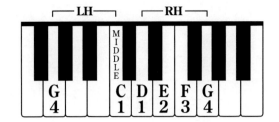

Words and Music by Tim Hughes
Arr. by Kowalchyk and Lancaster

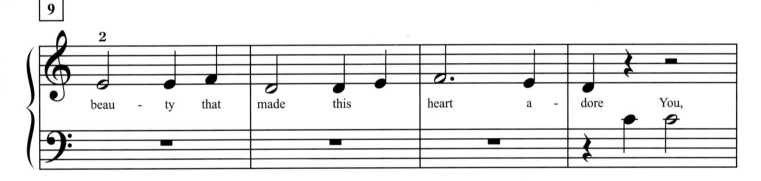

Duet Accompaniment: Student plays one octave higher.

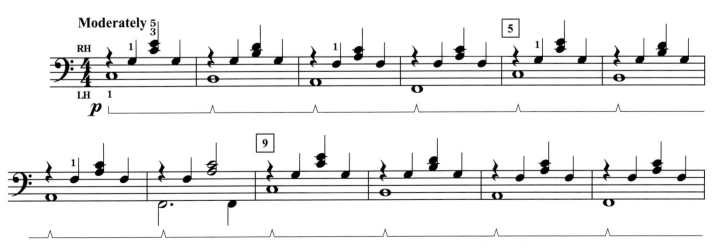

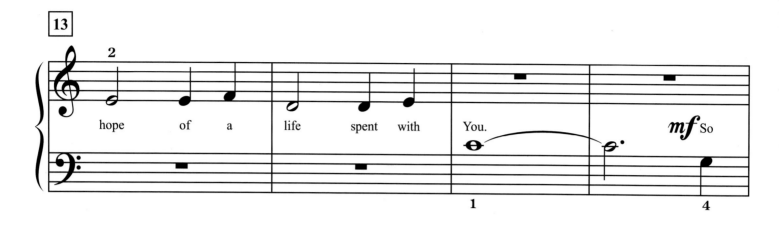

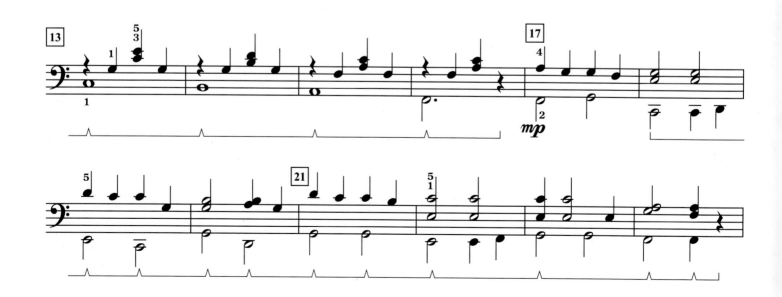

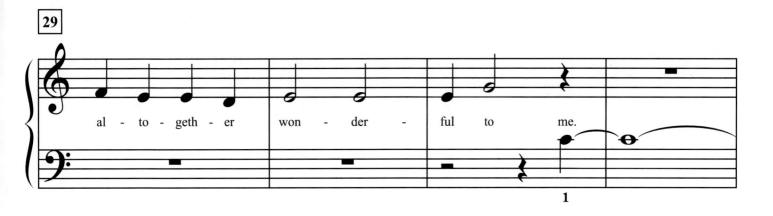

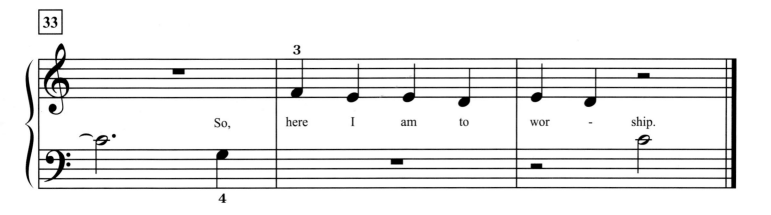

Shout to the North

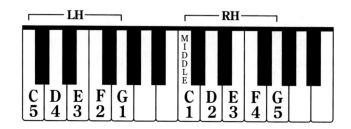

Words and Music by Martin Smith
Arr. by Kowalchyk and Lancaster

Flowing waltz tempo

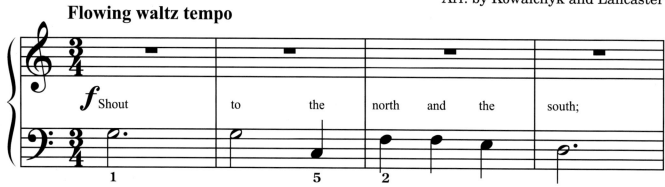

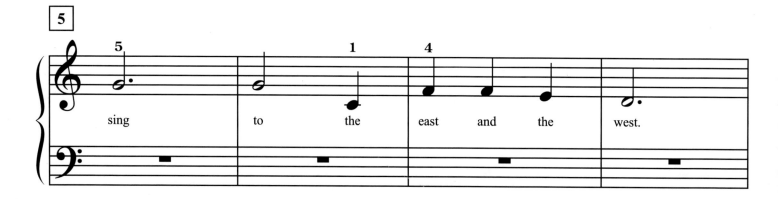

Duet Accompaniment: Student plays one octave higher.

Flowing waltz tempo

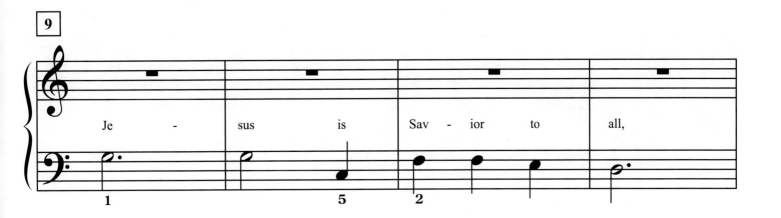

Je - sus is Sav - ior to all,

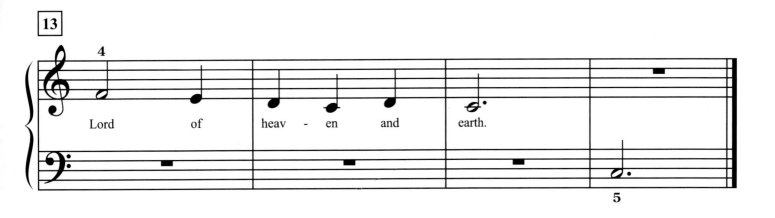

Lord of heav - en and earth.

Because He Lives

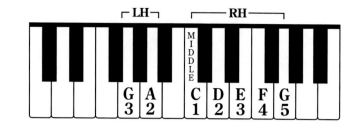

Words by William J. and Gloria Gaither
Music by William J. Gaither
Arr. by Kowalchyk and Lancaster

Duet Accompaniment: Student plays one octave higher.

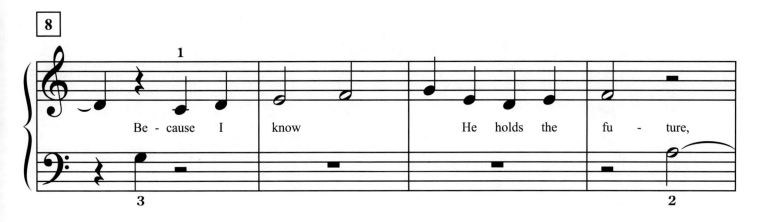

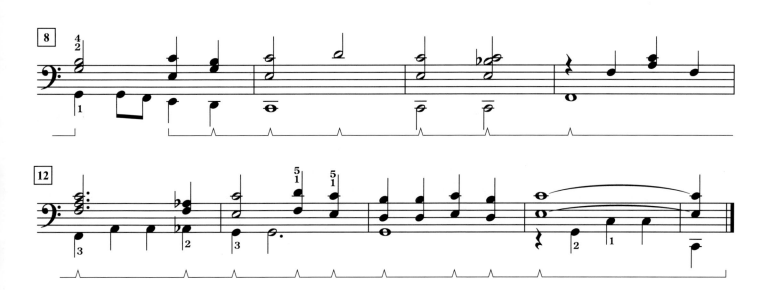

Worthy Is the Lamb

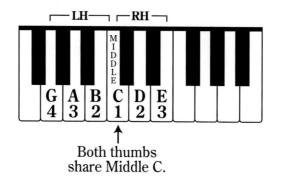

Both thumbs
share Middle C.

Words and Music by
Darlene Zschech
Arr. by Kowalchyk and Lancaster

Moderately

Wor - thy is the Lamb seat - ed on the throne.

Crown You now with man - y crowns, You reign vic - to - ri - ous.

Duet Accompaniment: Student plays one octave higher.

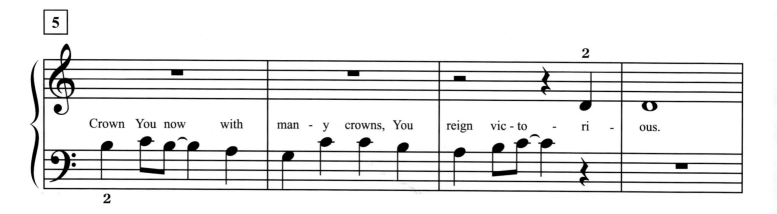

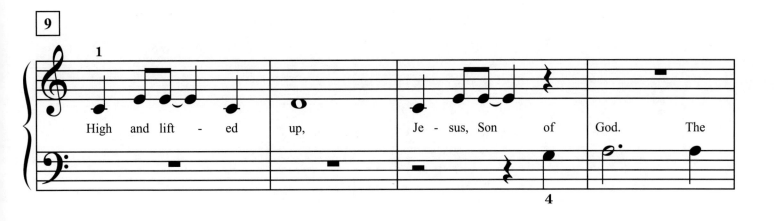

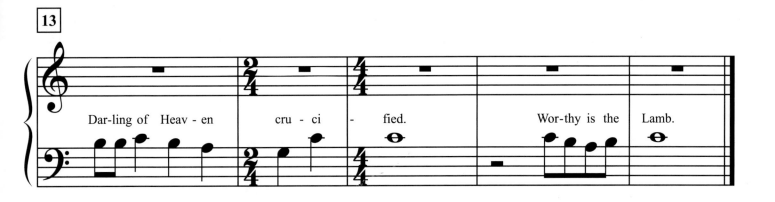

How Great Is Our God

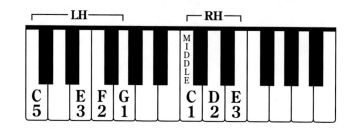

Words and Music by
Jesse Reeves, Chris Tomlin and Ed Cash
Arr. by Kowalchyk and Lancaster

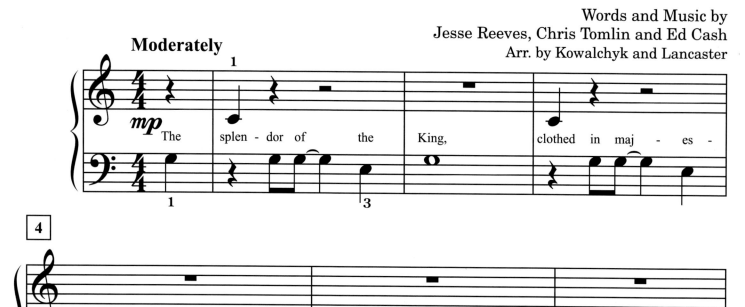

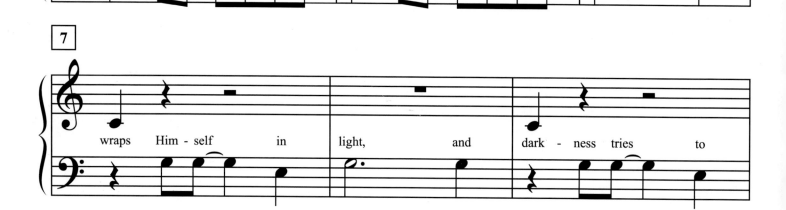

Duet Accompaniment: Student plays one octave higher.

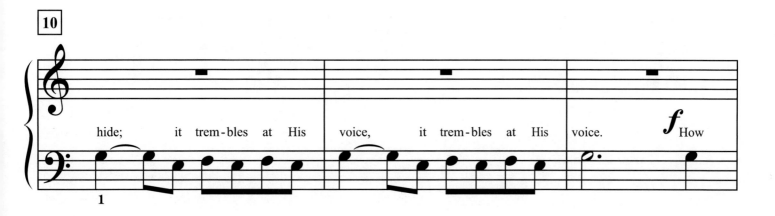

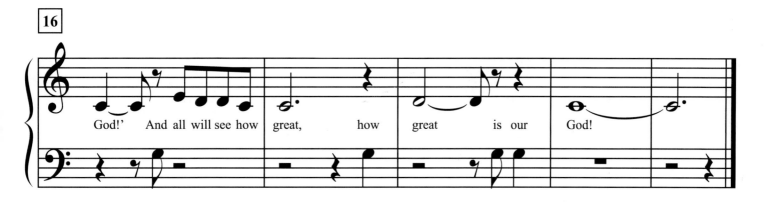

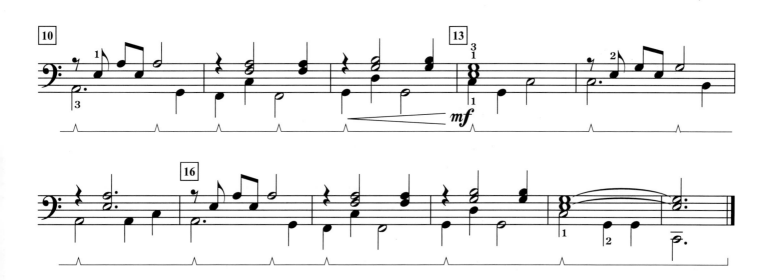

Lord, I Lift Your Name on High

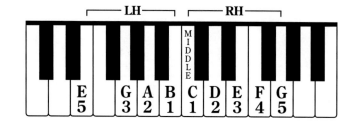

Words and Music by Rick Founds
Arr. by Kowalchyk and Lancaster

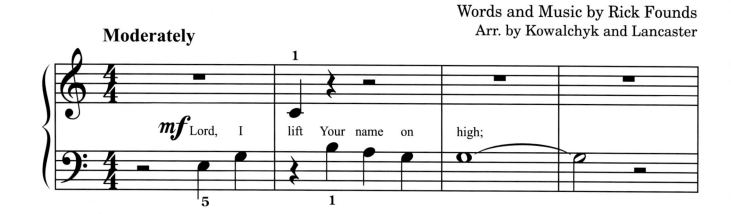

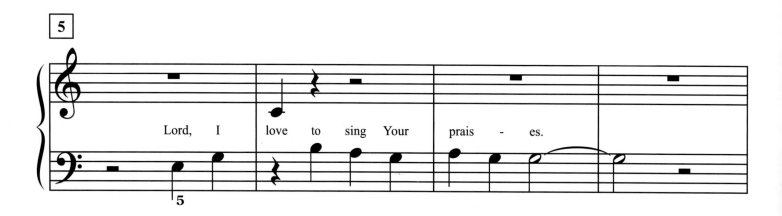

Duet Accompaniment: Student plays one octave higher.

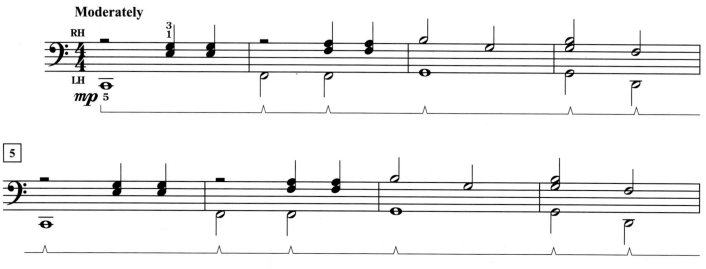

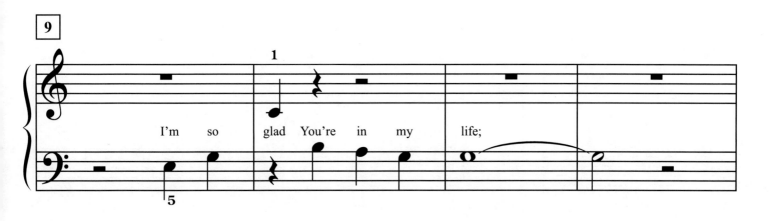

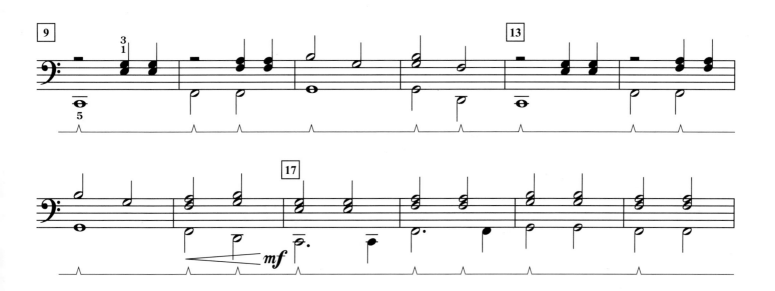

52

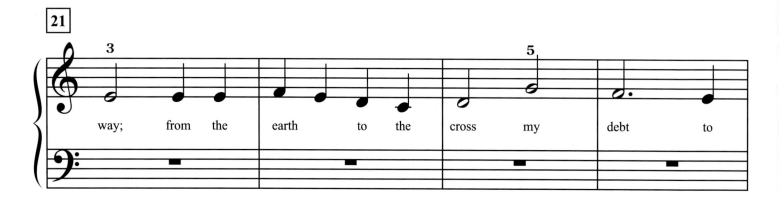

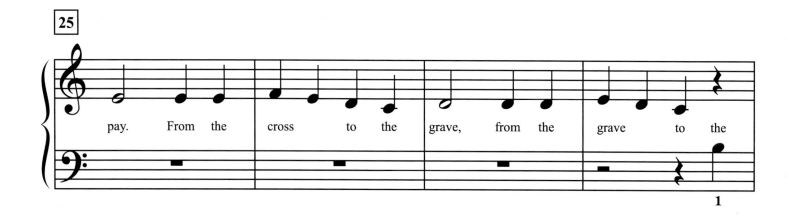

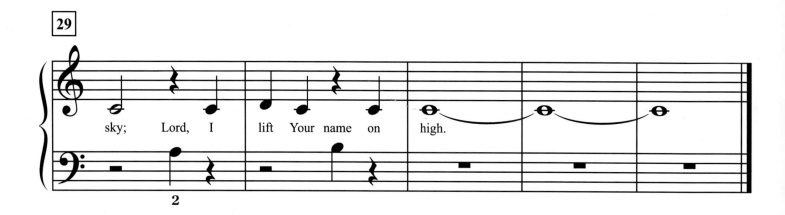

We Fall Down

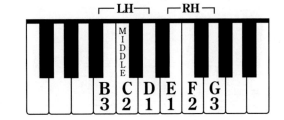

Words and Music by Chris Tomlin
Arr. by Kowalchyk and Lancaster

Moderately fast (in 2)

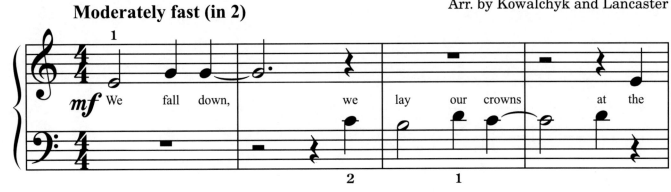

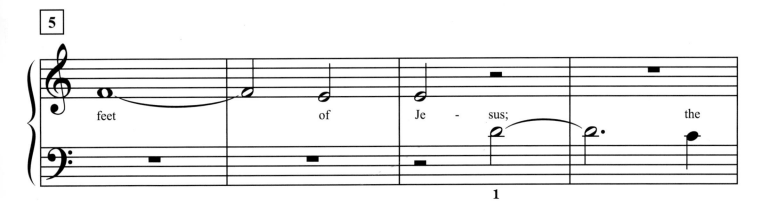

Duet Accompaniment: Student plays one octave higher.

Moderately fast (in 2)

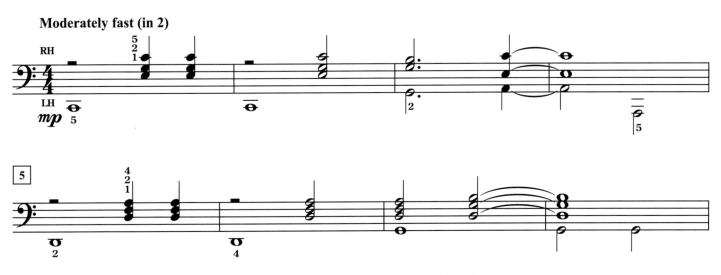

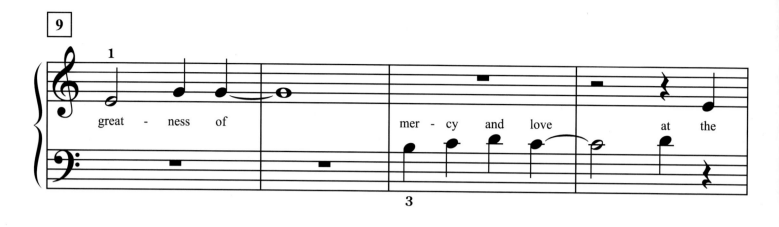

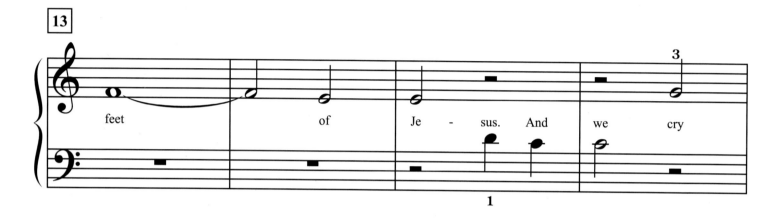

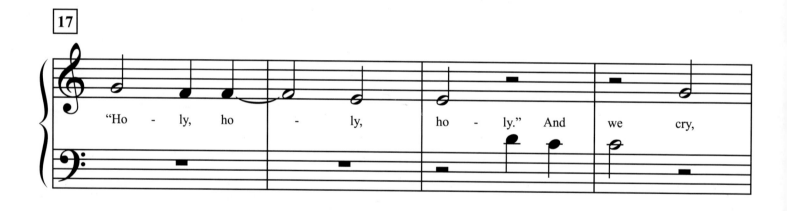

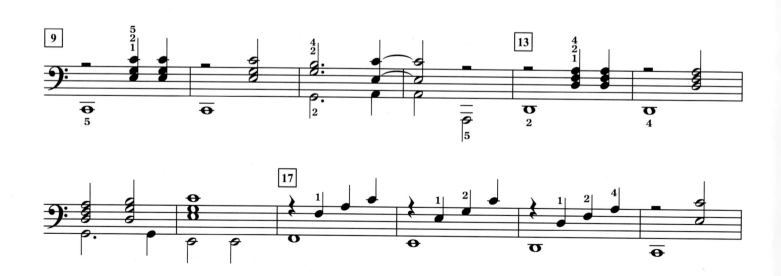

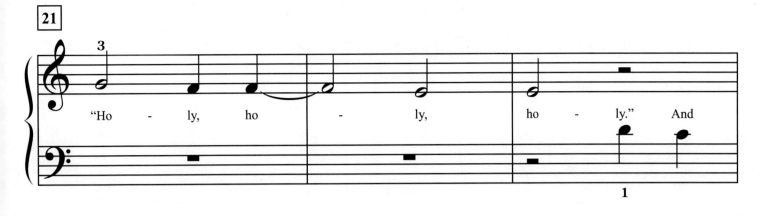

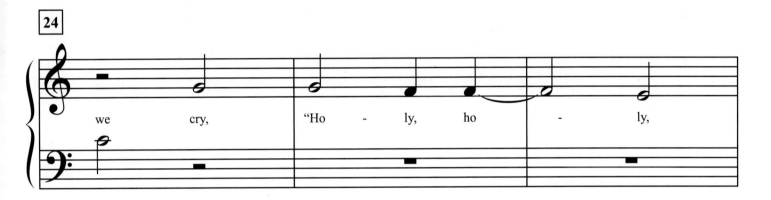

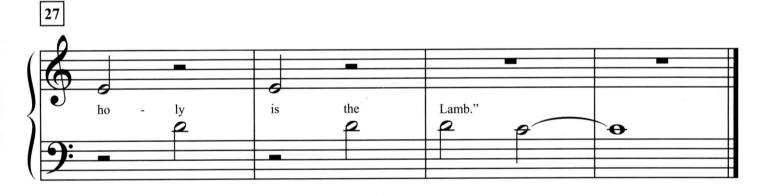

Mary, Did You Know?

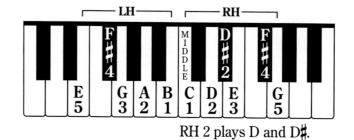

RH 2 plays D and D♯.

Words and Music by
Mark Lowry and Buddy Greene
Arr. by Kowalchyk and Lancaster

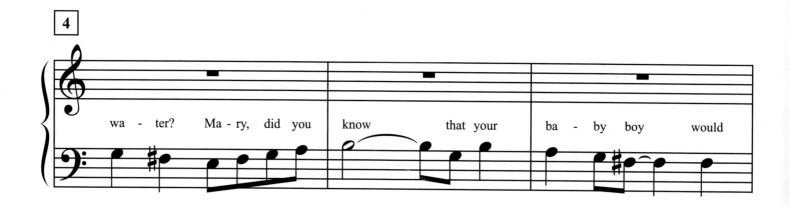

Duet Accompaniment: Student plays one octave higher.

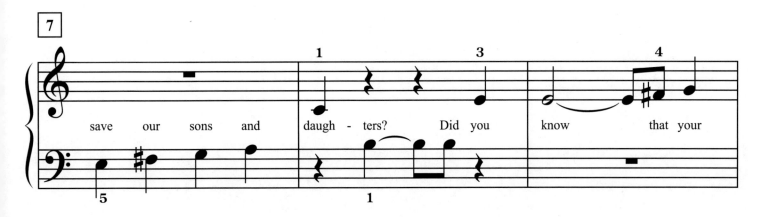

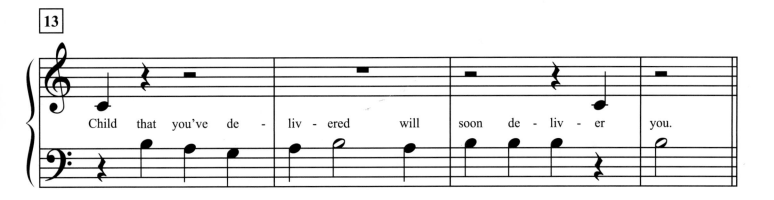

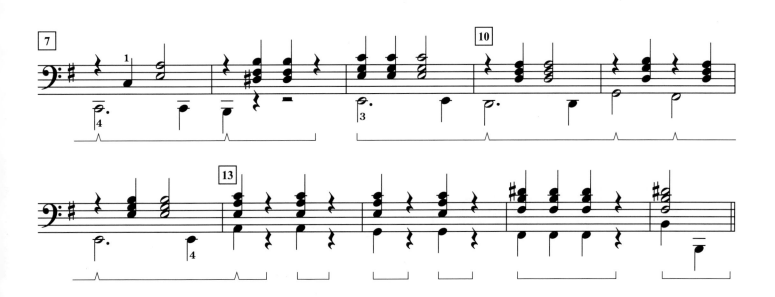

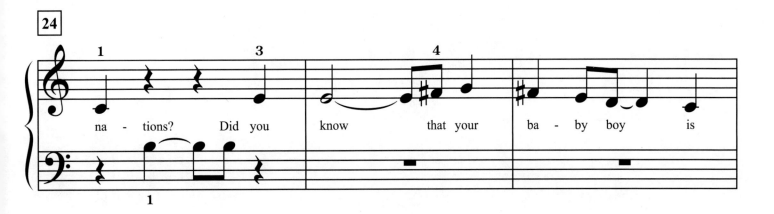

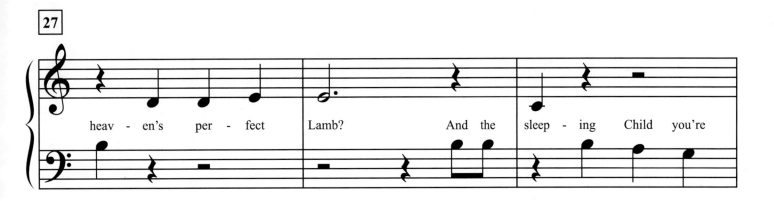

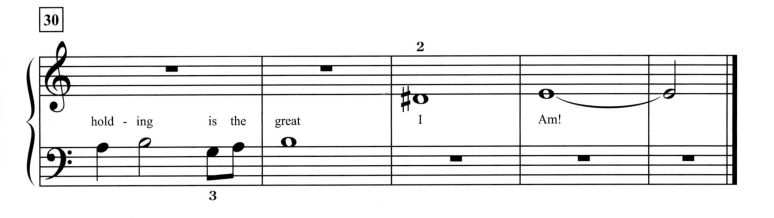

Winter Wonderland

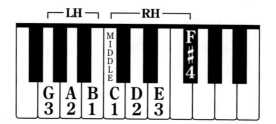

Words by Dick Smith
Music by Felix Bernard
Arr. by Kowalchyk and Lancaster

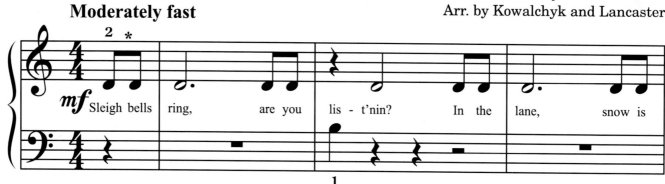

* Optional: Students may perform the pairs of eighth notes in swing style (♫ = ♪ ♪).

Duet Accompaniment: Student plays one octave higher.

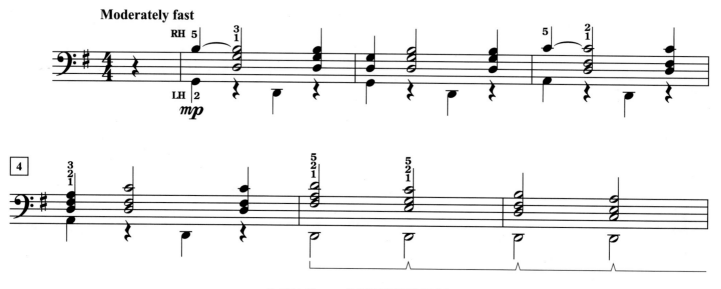

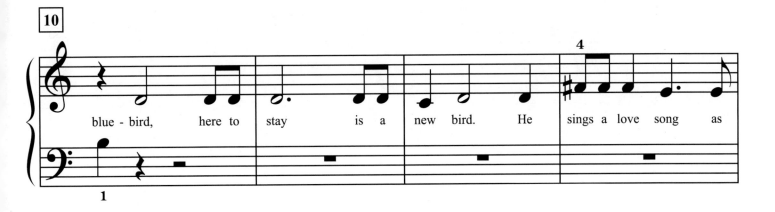

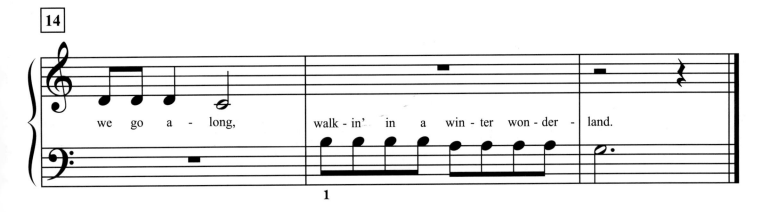

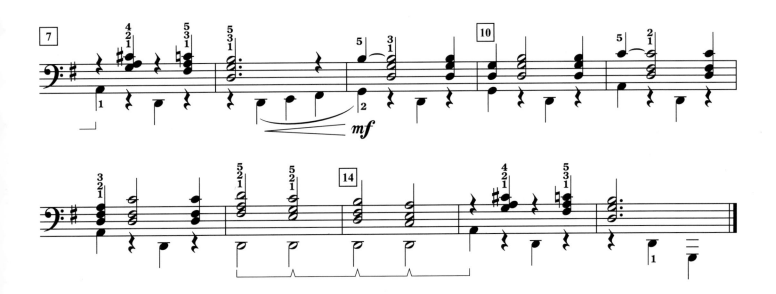

Sleigh Ride

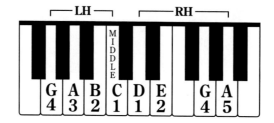

Music by Leroy Anderson
Words by Mitchell Parish
Arr. by Kowalchyk and Lancaster

With energy

Just hear those sleigh bells jin-gl-ing, ring-ting-tin-gl-ing, too.

Come on, it's love-ly weath-er for a sleigh ride to-geth-er with you.

Duet Accompaniment: Student plays one octave higher.

quarter notes detached throughout

With energy

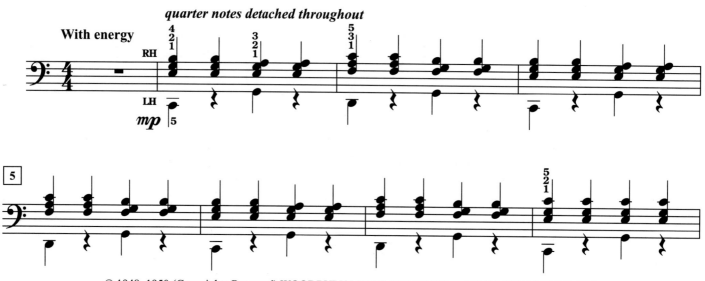

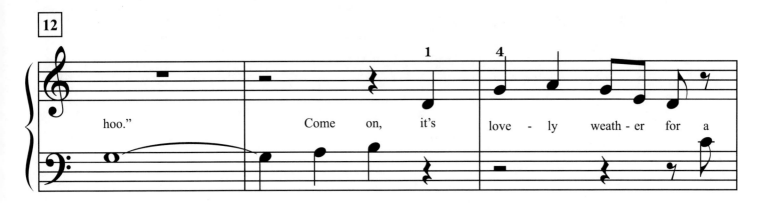

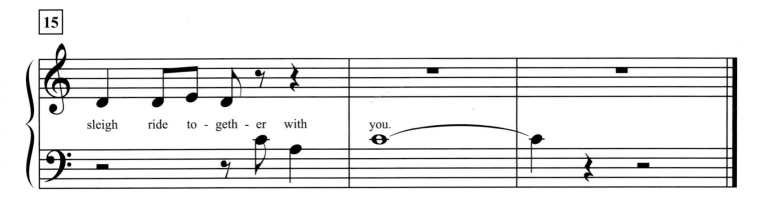

Frosty the Snowman

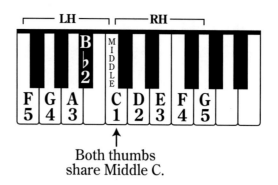

Both thumbs
share Middle C.

Words and Music by
Steve Nelson and Jack Rollins
Arr. by Kowalchyk and Lancaster

Moderately fast

Frost - y the Snow-man was a jol - ly, hap - py soul, with a
Frost - y the Snow-man is a fair - y tale they say, he was

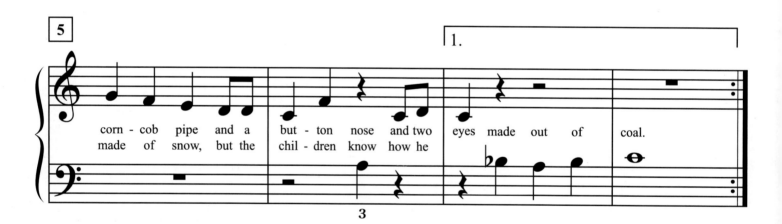

corn - cob pipe and a but - ton nose and two eyes made out of coal.
made of snow, but the chil - dren know how he

Duet Accompaniment: Student plays one octave higher.

Moderately fast

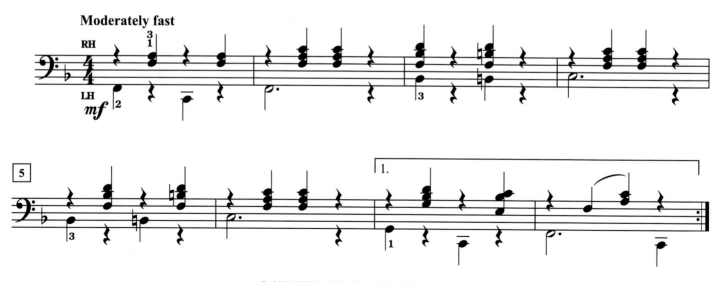

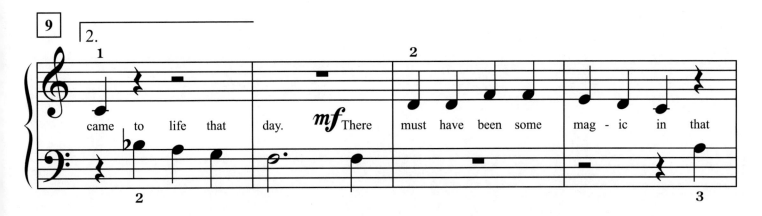

came to life that day. *mf* There must have been some mag - ic in that

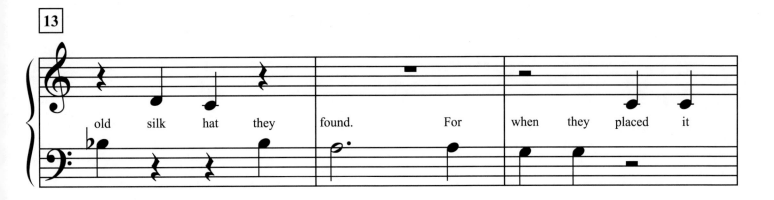

old silk hat they found. For when they placed it

on his head, he be - gan to dance a - round. *f* Oh,

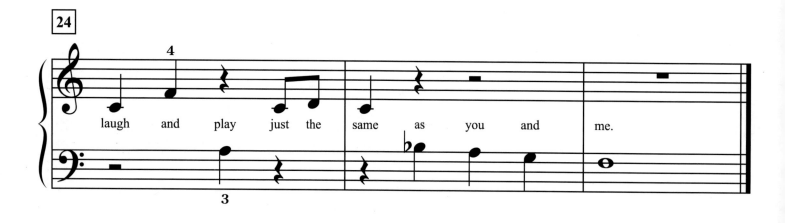

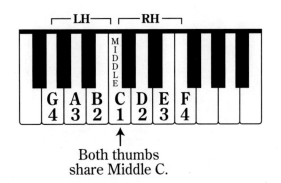

The Little Drummer Boy

Words and Music by
Harry Simeone, Henry Onorati and Katherine Davis
Arr. by Kowalchyk and Lancaster

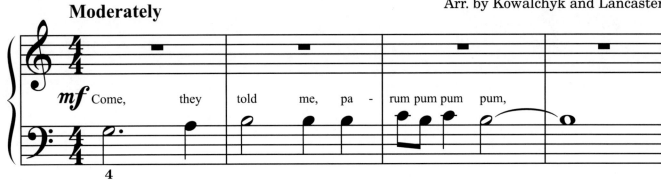

Come, they told me, pa - rum pum pum pum,

our new - born King to see, pa - rum pum pum pum.

Duet Accompaniment: Student plays one octave higher.

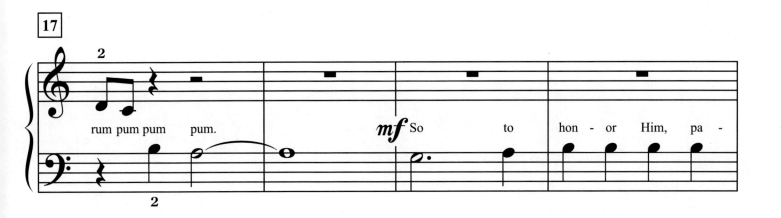

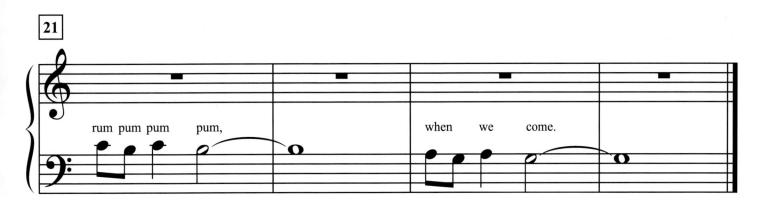

It's the Most Wonderful Time of the Year

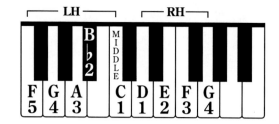

Words and Music by
Eddie Pola and George Wyle
Arr. by Kowalchyk and Lancaster

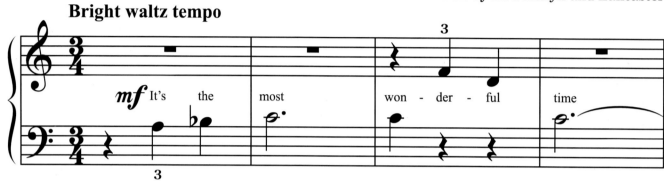

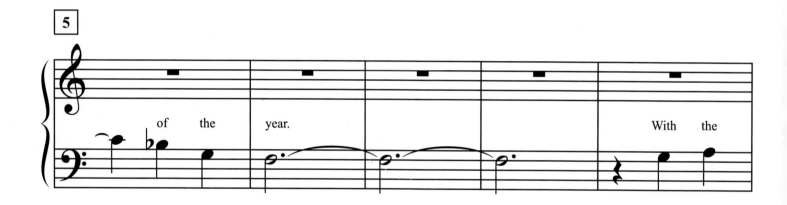

Duet Accompaniment: Student plays one octave higher.

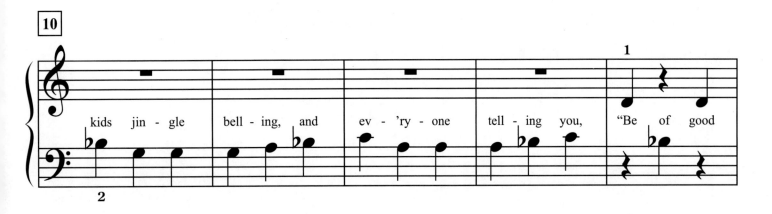

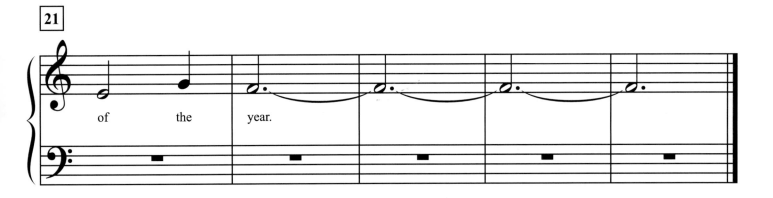

Santa Claus Is Comin' to Town

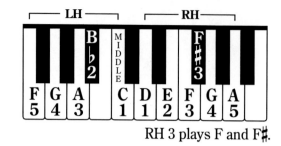

RH 3 plays F and F♯.

Words by Haven Gillespie
Music by J. Fred Coots
Arr. by Kowalchyk and Lancaster

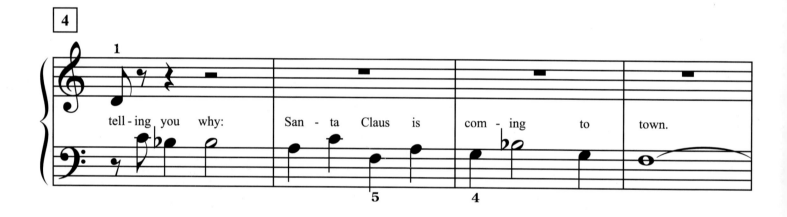

Duet Accompaniment: Student plays one octave higher.

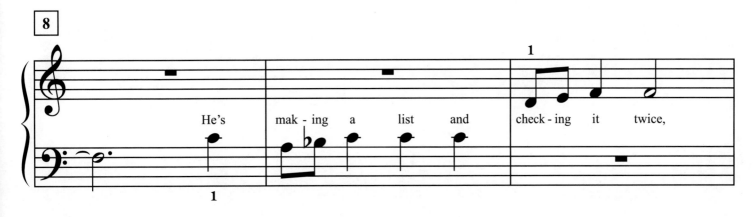

He's mak - ing a list and check - ing it twice,

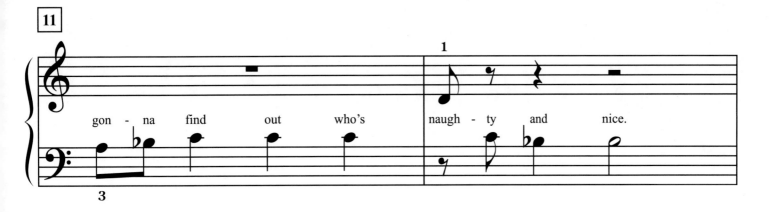

gon - na find out who's naugh - ty and nice.

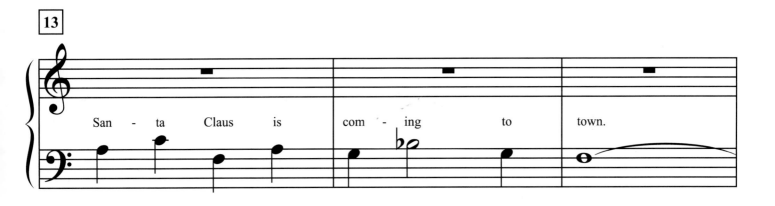

San - ta Claus is com - ing to town.

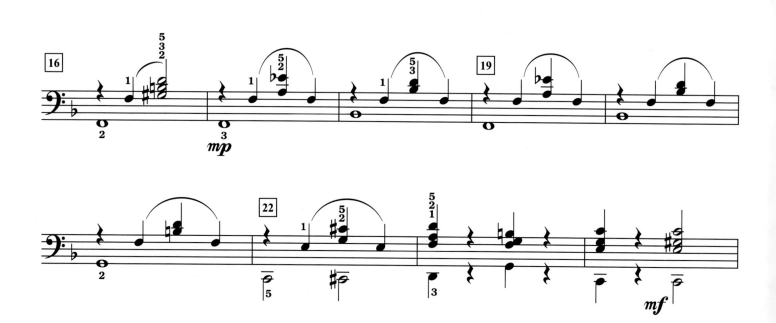

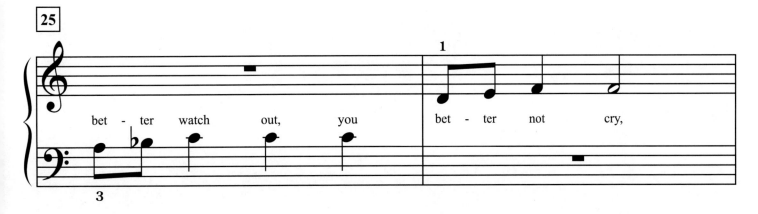

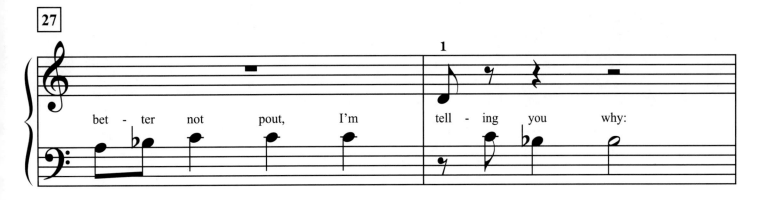

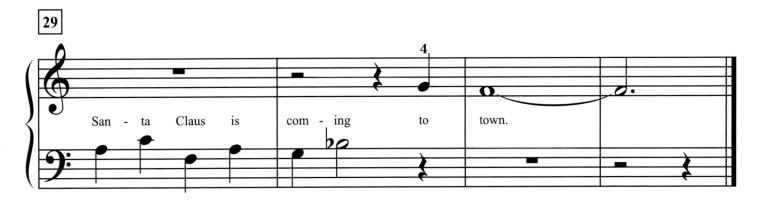

Let It Snow!
Let It Snow!
Let It Snow!

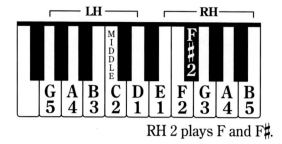

RH 2 plays F and F♯.

Words by Sammy Cahn
Music by Jule Styne
Arr. by Kowalchyk and Lancaster

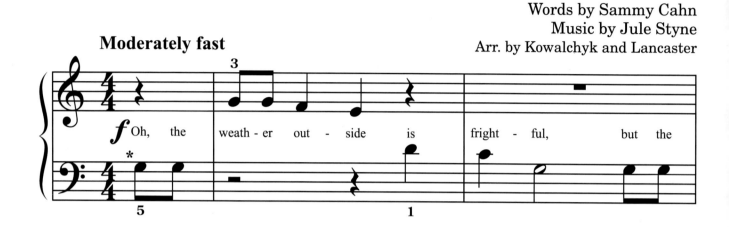

Oh, the weath-er out-side is fright-ful, but the

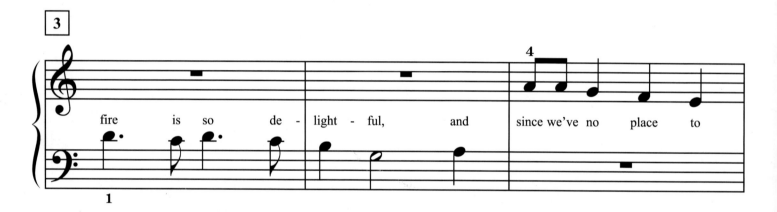

fire is so de-light-ful, and since we've no place to

* **Optional:** The pairs of eighth notes may be performed in swing style.

Duet Accompaniment: Student plays one octave higher.

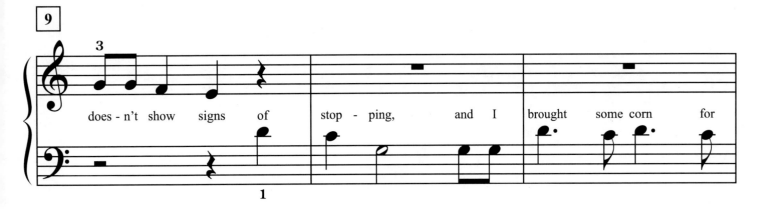

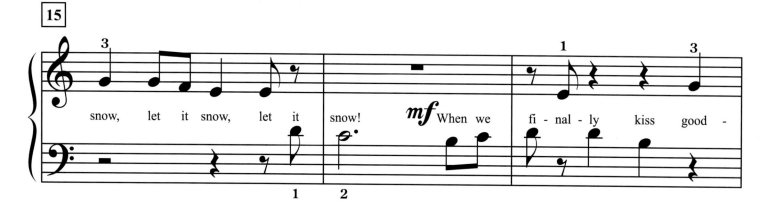

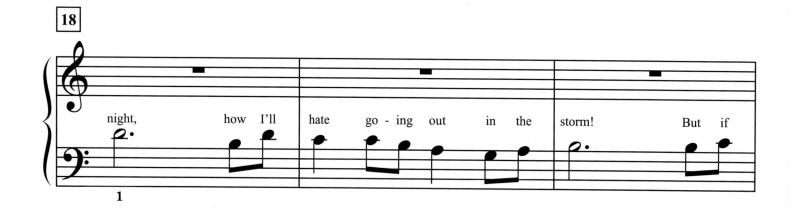

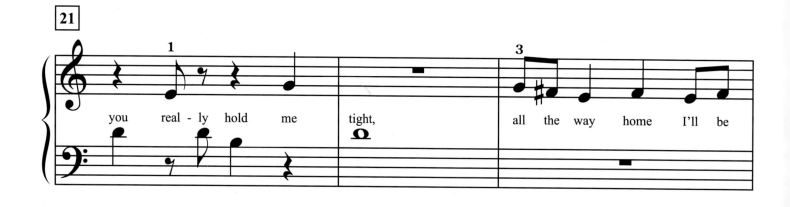

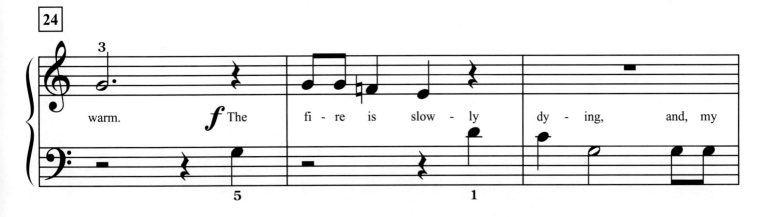

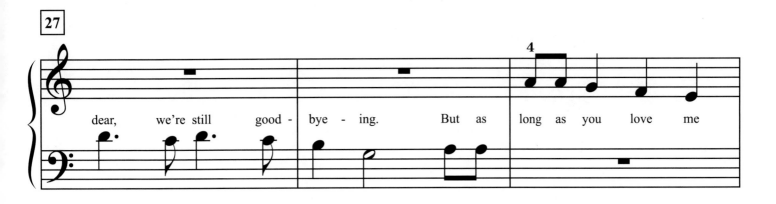